PIANO . VOCAL

VOLUME 1

THE VERNON DUKE SONGBOOK

Edited by Scott Dunn

Cover photo: Vernon Duke in England (1953).

ISBN 978-1-4584-1642-1

DISTRIBUTED BY

7777 W. BLUEMOUND RD. P.O. BOX 13819 MILWAUKEE, WI 53213

www.boosey.com
www.halleonard.com

FOREWORD

His early history reads like an epic novel. Vladimir Alexandrovitch Dukelsky (1903-1969) was born into a White Russian family at a railway station near Minsk. A child prodigy, he studied composition with Glière at the Kiev Conservatory. Forced into exile by the Bolshevik Revolution, he fled to Constantinople, where – pounding the keyboard at a local café – the international clientele demanded a remarkable American song called "Swanee." His first ballet was produced in 1921, shortly after which he emigrated to America, where he supported himself accompanying gypsy violinists and writing music for magic acts.

One day in 1923, the nineteen-year-old esthete had a couple of his modernist songs performed at a 'new music' concert. Nobody raised an ear – nobody, that is, except for the twenty-four-year-old composer of that self-same "Swanee." George Gershwin befriended "Dukie" – it was George himself who later came up with the Anglicized moniker "Vernon Duke" – and took him round to his publisher. The struggling Duke amassed a small bankroll preparing piano parts of some Gershwin tunes (including "Somebody Loves Me"), ghost-writing some ballet music for George, and arranging the piano solo version of *Rhapsody in Blue* (for which he received the lordly sum of $100). This was enough to enable Duke to sail for Paris in 1924. He wangled an invitation to play his as-yet-unperformed Piano Concerto for ballet impresario Sergei Diaghilev, and was immediately commissioned to compose a ballet for the Ballets Russes.

The twenty-one-year-old Dukelsky's *Zephyr et Flore* premiered in 1925, and his serious music career was underway. Still, he tried also to heed Gershwin's advice – "There's no money in that kind of stuff, try to write some real popular tunes" – and started interpolating songs into London musical comedies. On March 25th 1929, Duke's First Symphony was introduced by his mentor Serge Koussevitzky and the Boston Symphony, just about the same time he permanently moved back to America. Gershwin set him up with a budding lyricist pal of his brother Ira's, Yip Harburg, and Broadway had a new Russian composer.

Duke and Harburg's first break was with the 1932 revue *Walk a Little Faster*, starring Beatrice Lillie. Duke dashed off "April in Paris" on a battered speakeasy piano when sketch writer Robert Benchley mused "Oh, to be in Paris now that April's here." The Duke-Harburg partnership soon ran aground as the pair battled during the tryout of the *Ziegfeld Follies of 1934*. For the *Ziegfeld Follies of 1936*, Duke called on Ira Gershwin, then drifted through numerous lyricists for the rest of his career. He wrote three shows with John Latouche, including the 1940 Ethel Waters vehicle *Cabin in the Sky*, and three with Howard Dietz, including the ill-fated *Sadie Thompson*. Duke then joined with light verse master Ogden Nash for another three shows, beginning with the futuristic musical comedy *Sweet Bye and Bye* (1946). (The book was by S.J. Perelman and Al Hirschfeld; the show quickly shuttered in Philadelphia and Hirschfeld went back to drawing lines instead of writing lines.)

Duke was to straddle the serious and pop music fields throughout his career; he was the only Broadway composer who was a household fixture at the Gershwins and the Prokofievs. He specialized in highly complex Broadway art songs, what he referred to as his "out of this world" tunes. ("Not heavenly, just plain uncommercial.") Songs distinguished by constantly modulating keys and shifting harmonies, beneath strong closely chromatic melodies. This can be hard on a singer, and even harder on an audience looking for jingly tunes they can whistle all the way home. But Duke's intricacies resulted in richly textured, lush songs of great beauty. His four enduring hits – "April in Paris," "I Can't Get Started," "Taking a Chance on Love," and "Autumn in New York" – remain favorites of jazz musicians, but there is more to Duke's catalogue as is well demonstrated in this first volume of *The Vernon Duke Songbook* by such great forgotten ballads as "Born Too Late" and "Roundabout," as well as breezier items like "Good Little Girls" and "I Like the Likes of You" (which with it's slyly playful verse was a particular favorite of George Gershwin's).

Why has his name slipped into relative anonymity? First, the complexity of his songs has cut down on the frequency of performance. And unlike many of his contemporaries, Duke was never able to move into the modern book musical. Thus all but one of his shows are long forgotten. *Cabin in the Sky*, his first Broadway book musical, was a wartime hit; his other ten book musicals all failed, in most cases dismally. Clearly, Duke himself had a hand in his fate. One might well question his ability at project picking, not to mention his luck. And he was not necessarily an easy man to get along with; none of Duke's collaborations lasted long – even the affable Ira Gershwin couldn't work with his beloved brother's pal "Dukie" ("for geographical and other valid reasons" per V.D.). Accordingly, he spent his career going from lyricist to lyricist; working with nearly all of the best lyricists of his era, including Harold Rome, the great Johnny Mercer and the lyricists represented in this volume (Interestingly, several of his hits have lyrics by Duke himself, including the artful "Autumn in New York." Not bad for someone raised in Russia with English as his fourth language.)

Duke's work officially emerged from undeserved obscurity in 1999 when Nonesuch Records released the smashingly good *Dawn Upshaw Sings Vernon Duke* and his 1924 Piano Concerto was finally performed at Carnegie Hall. Ms. Upshaw's renditions introduced Duke to new generations of listeners. Now, with the publication of *The Vernon Duke Songbook*, Duke's "out of this world" tunes are here for us to explore – hour after hour – on our own piano.

Steven Suskin
(author of *Show Tunes, Second Act Trouble* and *The Sound of Broadway Music*)

CONTENTS

VERNON DUKE (Vladimir Dukelsky)
(1903–1969)

In 1903 Vladimir Alexandrovitch Dukelsky was born in a railway station near the village of Parfianovka, Russia. At age twelve he was admitted to the prestigious Kiev Conservatory to study composition with Reinhold Glière. Glière's most celebrated protégé, Sergei Prokofiev, though twelve years older than Dukelsky, eventually became a life-long friend and mentor to the younger composer. In 1920, Dukelsky, his widowed mother, and brother Alexis, fled the Bolshevik Revolution – spending two years in Constantinople before emigrating to the United States and arriving in New York City in 1922.

In New York, Arthur Rubinstein and George Gershwin took an interest in Dukelsky's talent. Rubinstein asked the nineteen-year-old composer to write for him a 'one-movement piano concerto, pianistically grateful and not too cerebral'. Both Gershwin and Rubinstein liked the new work; Gershwin would often ask Dukelsky to play its lyrical second theme at parties and Rubinstein promised to perform it (a promise not kept through no fault of Rubinstein's).

Dukelsky arrived in Paris the summer of 1924, with plans to orchestrate his Piano Concerto in C, secure its premiére and 'find his musical way'. He soon met Serge Koussevitzky, who offered Dukelsky a music publishing contract, and Serge Diaghilev, who upon hearing the new piano concerto played by the composer engaged Dukelsky to compose a new ballet for his Ballets Russes. For Diaghilev, Dukelsky composed *Zephyr et Flore*, which was presented in Paris and Monte Carlo in 1925 with a scenario by Boris Kochno, sets by Georges Braque, choreography by Leonide Massine, and costumes by Coco Chanel.

Dukelsky subsequently produced several ballets and a distinguished body of concert music: his First Symphony was premiered by Koussevitzky and the Boston Symphony in 1928; in 1931, *Epitaph* (for Diaghilev) again with Koussevitzky and Boston; in 1937 his Second Symphony in Paris; in 1938, his *The End of St Petersburg* oratorio premiered at Carnegie Hall; and finally, again with Koussevitzky and Boston, his 1943 Violin Concerto and his 1946 Cello Concerto (with Piatigorsky).

When Dukelsky became fascinated with writing for the London and Broadway stages, his good friend George Gershwin suggested he abbreviate his name to 'Vernon Duke'. As Vernon Duke, he contributed to more than seventeen West End and Broadway shows and worked with such distinguished lyricists as Ira Gershwin, Yip Harburg, Sammy Cahn, Ogden Nash and John Latouche. A number of his songs such as "April in Paris," "Autumn in New York," "I Can't Get Started" and "Taking a Chance on Love" were huge hits and have become standards of jazz and American popular song. His most notable Broadway success was the 1940 hit *Cabin in the Sky* with an all black cast, starring Ethel Waters, and choreography by George Balanchine.

During World War II, he served as a commissioned officer in the Coast Guard and for the Coast Guard wrote a touring fund-raising show which was also made into a movie in 1946 starring Sid Caesar, Janet Blair and Alfred Drake.

After the war, Duke returned to Paris where Roland Petit commissioned him to write a hugely successful, jazzy ballet called *Le Bal de Blanchisseuses* (*The Washer Women's Ball*) which received more than one hundred performances. About this same time his Third Symphony premiered in Brussels.

After several years of living between New York and Paris, Vernon Duke moved to Los Angeles in 1953 when Warner Brothers hired him to write scores for several musical films (including one, based on Duke's 1932 hit, called *April in Paris*). During this time Duke also wrote and published his autobiography *Passport to Paris*, as well as four books of poetry in Russian. Additionally he worked on several Broadway projects; wrote art songs; composed concert and chamber music; and revised many of his early concert works, including a Diaghilev commissioned opera called *Mistress into Maid*. Based on a charming Pushkin story, the opera is yet to be produced.

In Los Angeles, he was finally reunited with his beloved brother Alexis. He loved spending holidays with Alexis, his wife Romona and their daughter Natasha. Alexis worked as an artist at Metro-Goldwyn-Mayer; Natasha has had a distinguished career as an animator for Disney Studios.

In 1957 Duke married the American soprano, Kay McCracken who had been a student of the great Lotte Lehmann. She and Duke traveled and performed extensively together in concerts and recitals throughout the United States. Vernon Duke died in Santa Monica, California in January, 1969.

In 1998, the American pianist and conductor, Scott Dunn received permission to finish the long neglected Piano Concerto in C. Working from the published two-piano score, Dunn orchestrated the entire work in time for the official Gershwin Centennial concerts of 1999, where the concerto finally had its premiére at Carnegie Hall with the American Composers Orchestra, its orchestrator at the piano and Dennis Russell Davies conductor. In 2005 the concerto was recorded by Dunn in Moscow for NAXOS with Dimitry Yablonsky, conductor and the Russian Philharmonic Orchestra. (The recording also features the Duke Cello Concerto with cellist Sam Magill.)

Duke's reputation has continued its resurgence abroad and into the new century. In the fall of 2011, after extensive reconstruction, three of Dukelsky's major concert works – *The End of St Petersburg* oratorio; *Epitaph* (for Diaghilev) for orchestra, soprano and chorus; and *Dedicaces* for orchestra, piano solo and soprano obligato - were 'premiered' to great acclaim in Russia at the Philharmonia in St. Petersburg by the St. Petersburg Philharmonic, the Capella Choir, and various soloists of the Mariinsky Theatre with Dunn conducting.

Scott Dunn and Kay Duke Ingalls

February 2012

Ages Ago

from the play *Time Remembered*

Words and Music by
VERNON DUKE

lieved in love _____ But that was ag - es and ag - es a -

go. And still I try, now that I am de -

ceived in love _____ To stop the clock and re - cap - ture the

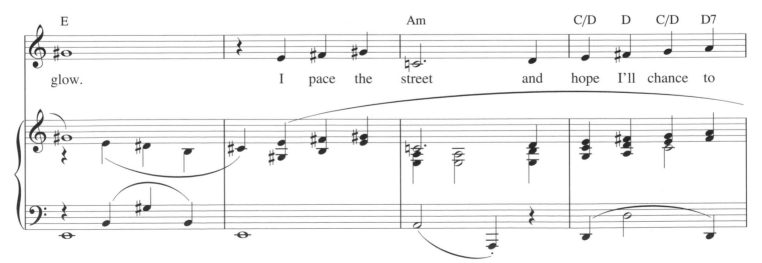

glow. I pace the street and hope I'll chance to

meet some - one I could com - plete - ly and mad - ly a -

dore. But I can't change, there's no dan - ger, be -

cause I know _____ I love the {girl}{boy} I loved ag - es a -

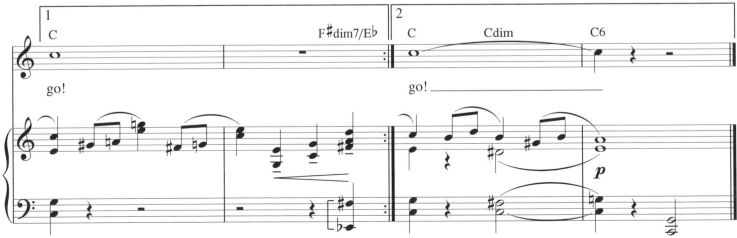

go! go! _____

April in Paris

from the Musical Revue *Walk a Little Faster*

Words by
E.Y. "YIP" HARBURG

Music by
VERNON DUKE

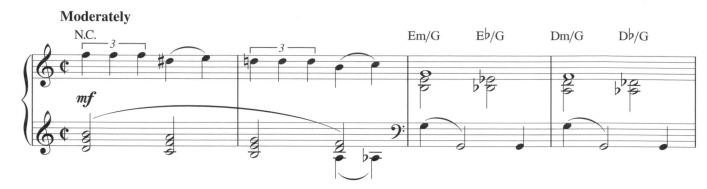

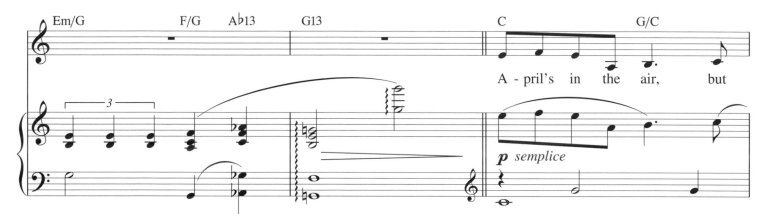

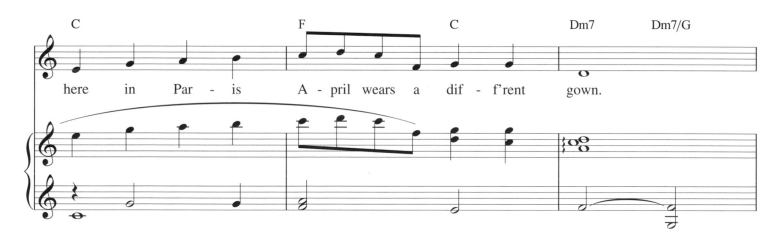

wine is in the air, I'm drunk with all the hap-pi-ness that Spring can give.

Nev-er dreamed it could be so ex-cit-ing to live.

A-pril in Par-is, _____ chest-nuts in blos-som, _

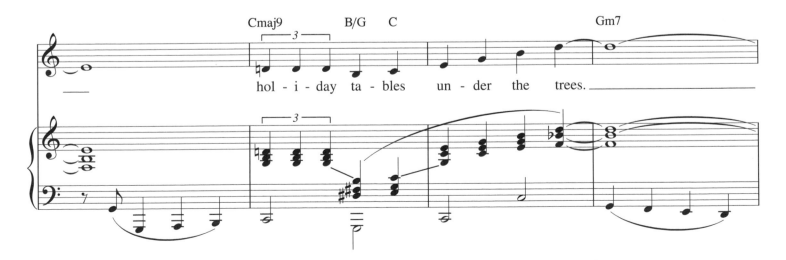

hol-i-day ta-bles un-der the trees. _____

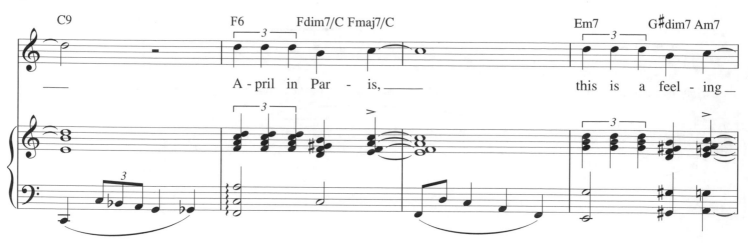

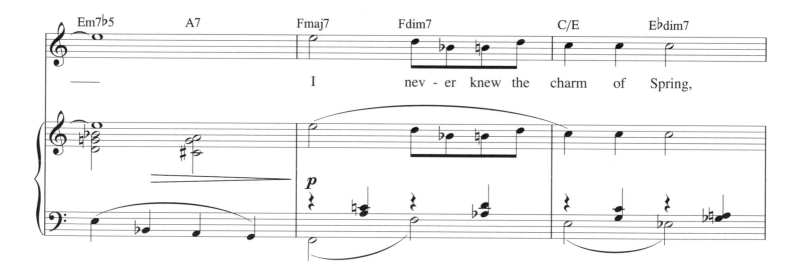

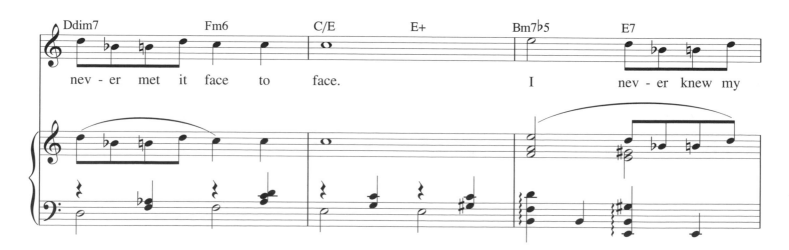

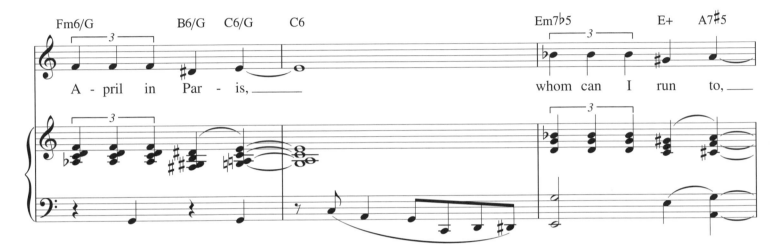

Autumn in New York

from the Musical Revue *Thumbs Up*

Words and Music by
VERNON DUKE

Slowly, poco rubato

It's time to end my lone-ly hol-i-day ___ and bid the coun-try a has-ty fare-well. So on this gray and mel-an-chol-y day I'll move ___ to a Man-hat-tan ho-tel. I'll dis-

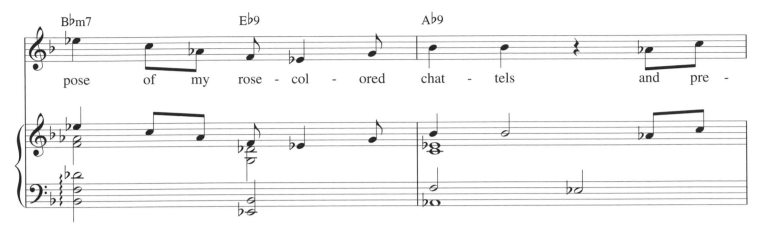

pose of my rose - col - ored chat - tels and pre -

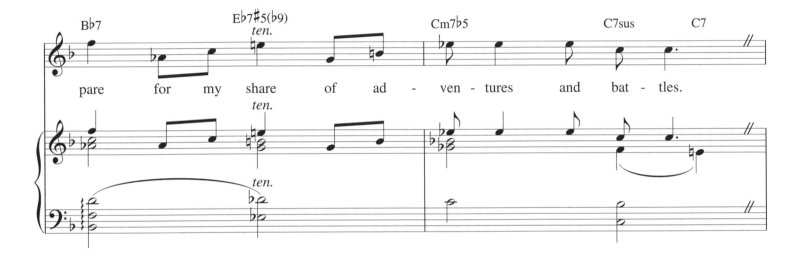

pare for my share of ad - ven - tures and bat - tles.

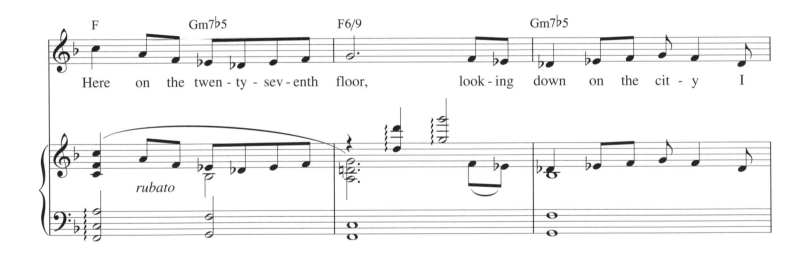

Here on the twen - ty - sev - enth floor, look - ing down on the cit - y I

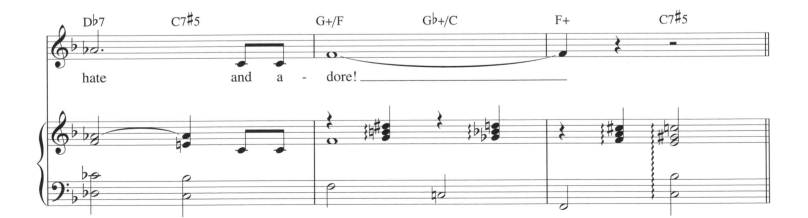

hate and a - dore!

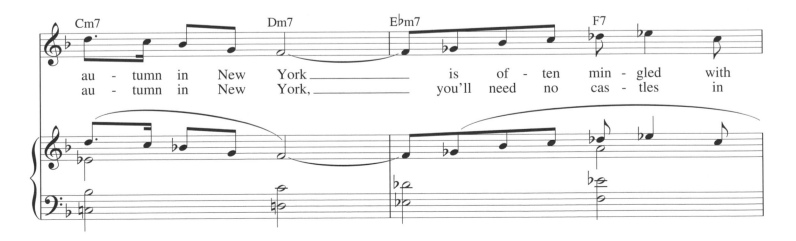

pain. _____
Spain. _____

Dream-ers with emp - ty
Lov - ers that bless the

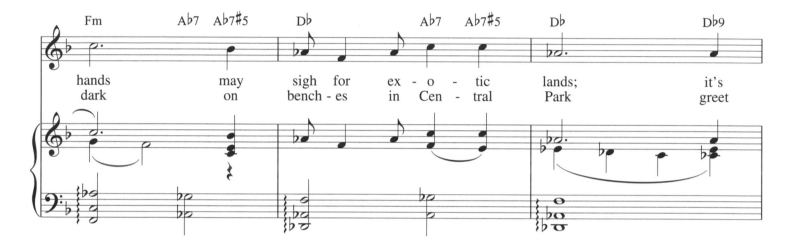

hands may sigh for ex - o - tic lands; it's
dark on bench - es in Cen - tral Park greet

au - tumn in New York, _____ it's good to live it a - gain.
au - tumn in New York; _____ it's good to live it a -

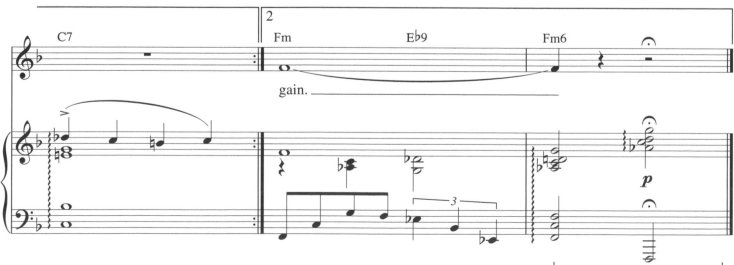

gain. _____

Born Too Late

from the Musical Comedy Production *Sweet Bye and Bye*

Words by
OGDEN NASH

Music by
VERNON DUKE

Languido

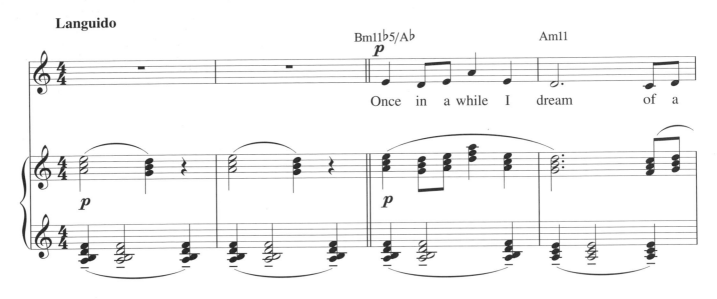

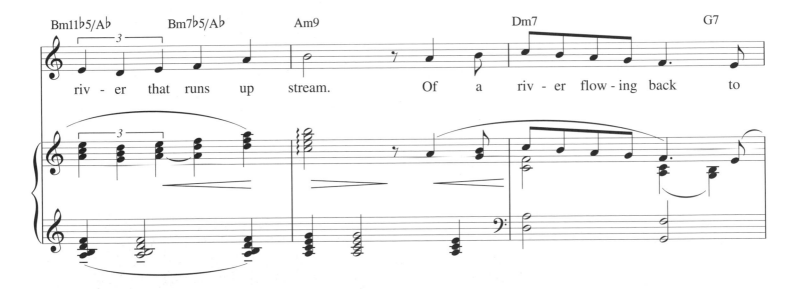

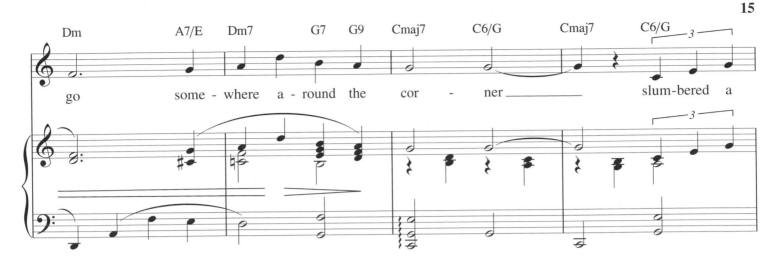

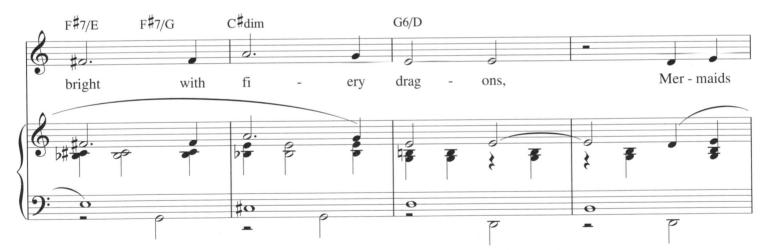

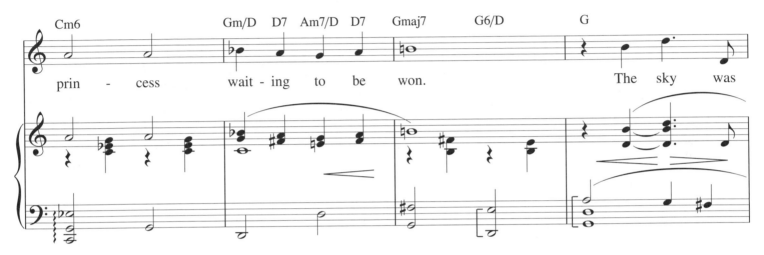

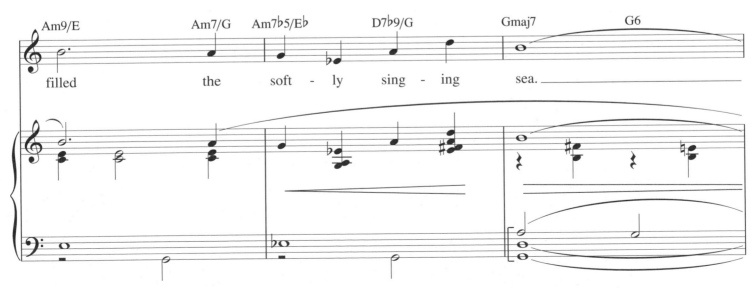

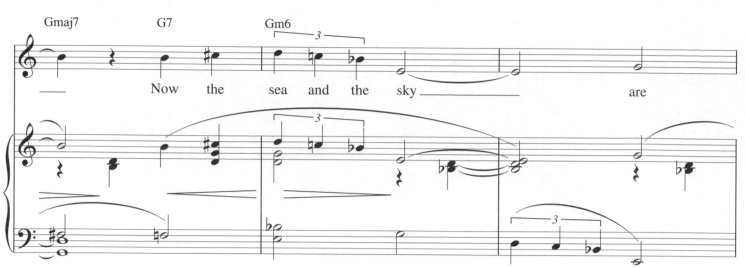

Now the sea and the sky _____ are

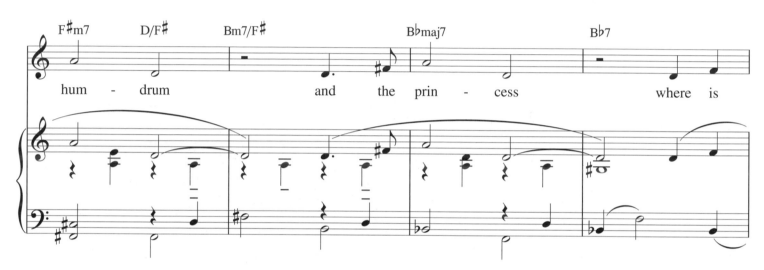

hum - drum and the prin - cess where is

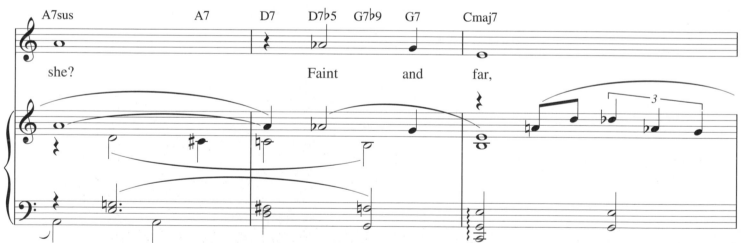

she? Faint and far, I can hear the mu - sic fade and

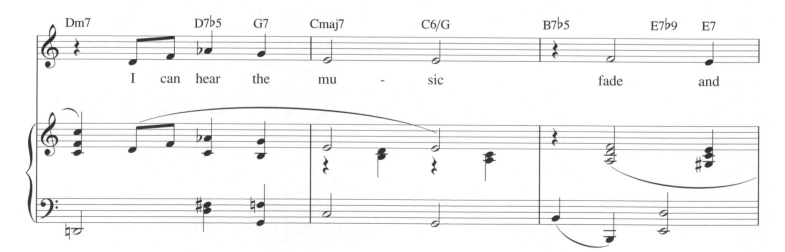

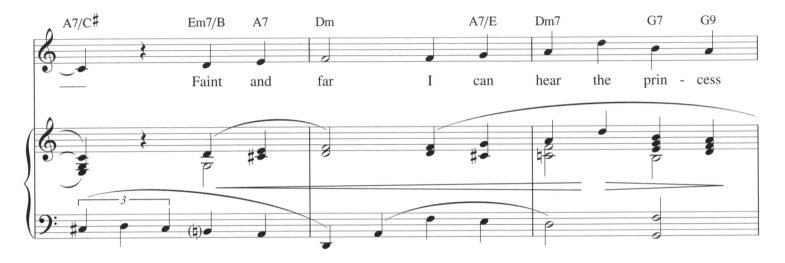

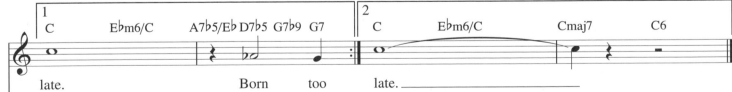

Good Little Girls

from the Musical Revue *Two's Company*

Words by
SAMMY CAHN

Music by
VERNON DUKE

co - rum.___ How - ev - er, take the one in the pet - it point frame, The em-

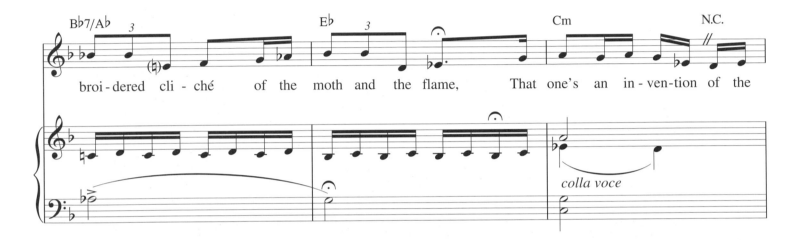

broi - dered cli - ché of the moth and the flame, That one's an in - ven - tion of the

colla voce

blue nose hi - er - ar - chy And as far as I'm con-cerned it's a bunch of Ma - lar - key! ___

Refrain
Lively one-step

I don't want me a poor___ young me - chan - ic,___ Not as
make Mis - ter X.___ quite ec - stat - ic,___ He has
be a sub - ur - ban com - mut - er,___ Not as

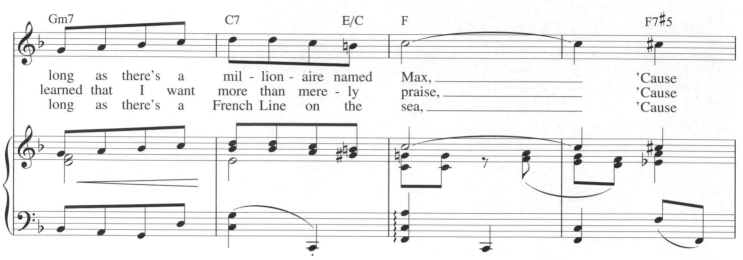

long as there's a mil - lion - aire named Max,_____ 'Cause
learned that I want more than mere - ly praise,_____ 'Cause
long as there's a French Line on the sea,_____ 'Cause

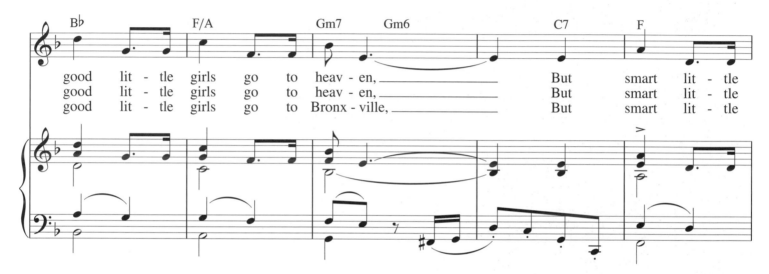

good lit - tle girls go to heav - en,_____ But smart lit - tle
good lit - tle girls go to heav - en,_____ But smart lit - tle
good lit - tle girls go to Bronx - ville,_____ But smart lit - tle

girls go to Berg - dorf's, to Bul - lock's, to Bon - wit's, to
girls go to Van Cleef and Ar - pels, to Tif - f'ny's and
girls go to Deau - ville, to Trou - ville, to Na - ples, to

Mag - nin's and Saks._____ When the rent's due I don't____
to Car - ti - er's._____ When he leaves me the part -
Nice and Ca - pri._____ I have learned how to han -

C7 F Gm7

start to pan - ic, _____ 'Cause I've got a land - lord
- ing's dra - mat - ic, _____ I shed tears you could - n't
- dle a suit - or, _____ He hands o - ver if he

C7 E/C F F7#5 Bb

I've taught to re - lax, _____ Oh, good lit - tle
get from Hel - en Hayes, _____ Oh, good lit - tle
wants to han - dle me. _____ For good lit - tle

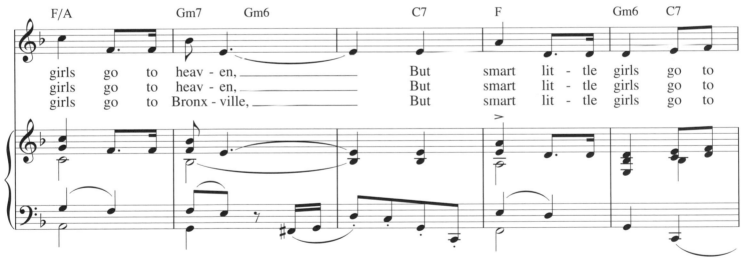

F/A Gm7 Gm6 C7 F Gm6 C7

girls go to heav - en, _____ But smart lit - tle girls go to
girls go to heav - en, _____ But smart lit - tle girls go to
girls go to Bronx - ville, _____ But smart lit - tle girls go to

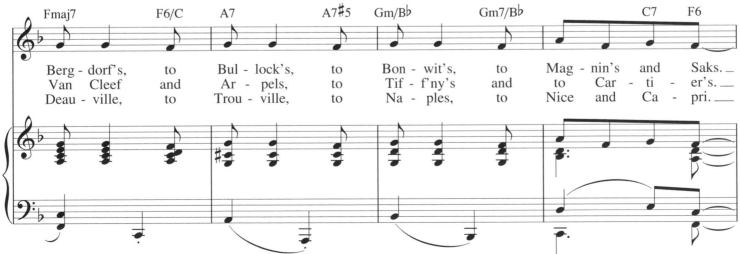

Fmaj7 F6/C A7 A7#5 Gm/Bb Gm7/Bb C7 F6

Berg - dorf's, to Bul - lock's, to Bon - wit's, to Mag - nin's and Saks. __
Van Cleef and Ar - pels, to Tif - f'ny's and to Car - ti - er's. __
Deau - ville, to Trou - ville, to Na - ples, to Nice and Ca - pri. __

I Am Only Human After All

from *The Garrick Gaieties*

Words by IRA GERSHWIN
and E.Y. "YIP" HARBURG

Music by
VERNON DUKE

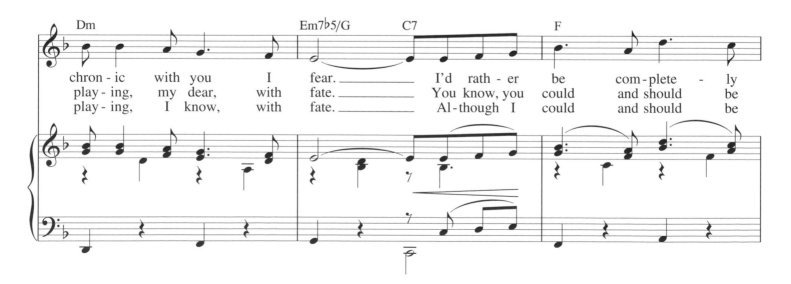

I Like the Likes of You

from *Ziegfeld Follies of 1934*

Lyric by
E.Y. "YIP" HARBURG

Music by
VERNON DUKE

I'm from Con-nect - i -cut. You see the state _ that I'm in,

I mean I'm in a mess. What was that speech, oh, yes, yes.

I like the likes of you, I like the things you do.

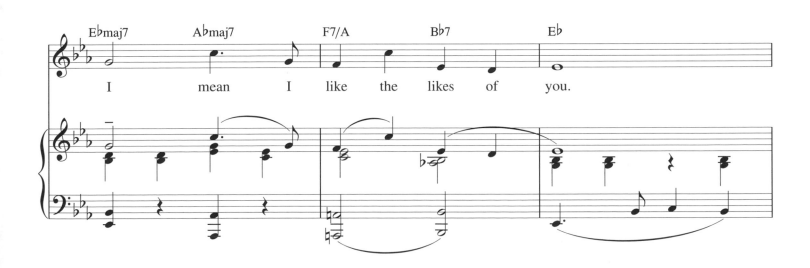

I mean I like the likes of you.

I like your eyes of blue, I think they're blue, don't

you? I mean I like your eyes of blue.

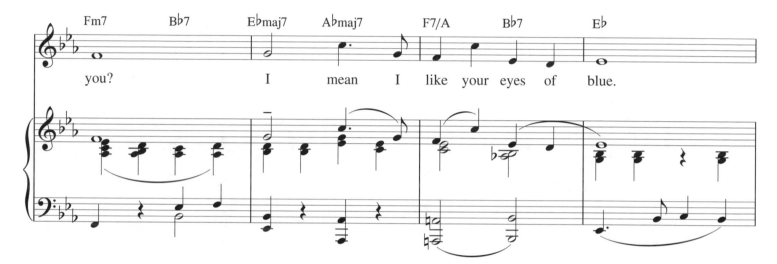

Oh, dear, _____ if I could on - ly say _ what I

mean, _____ I mean if I could mean what I say. _____ That is, I

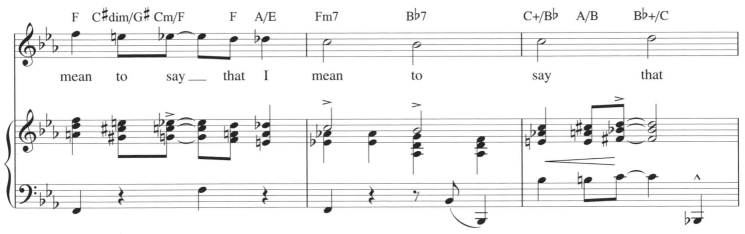

mean to say___ that I mean to say that

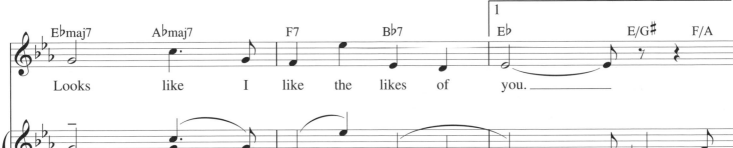

I like the likes of you. Your looks are pure de - luxe.

Looks like I like the likes of you. ___

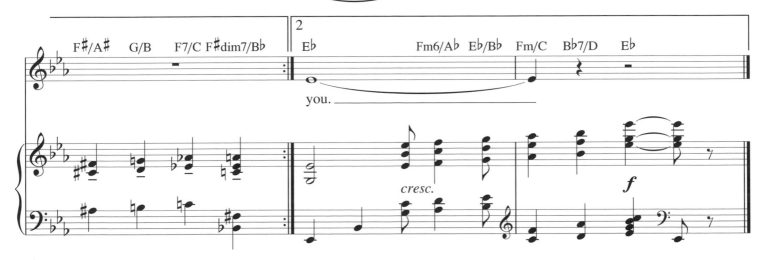

you. ___

Just Like a Man
from the Musical Comedy Production *Sweet Bye and Bye*

Words by
OGDEN NASH

Music by
VERNON DUKE

This page left blank to facilitate page turns.

Just Like Children
from *The Pink Jungle*

Words and Music by
VERNON DUKE

hib - it - ed babes in the wood! _____

poco rit. (Dance)

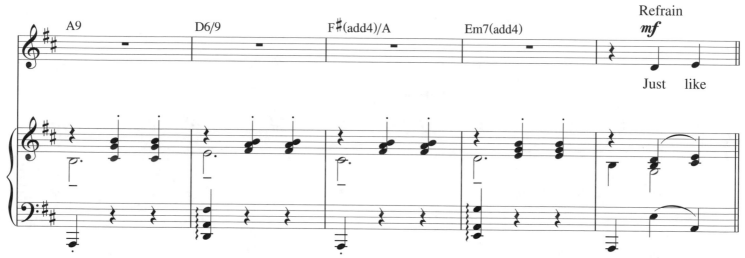

Refrain

Just like

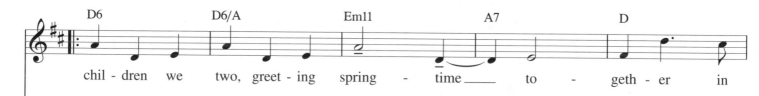

chil - dren we two, greet - ing spring - time _____ to - geth - er in

Cen - tral Park. _____ Let's be chil - dren, it's Rid - ing - The -

lightly

Swing time ___ An old _____ fash - ioned lark

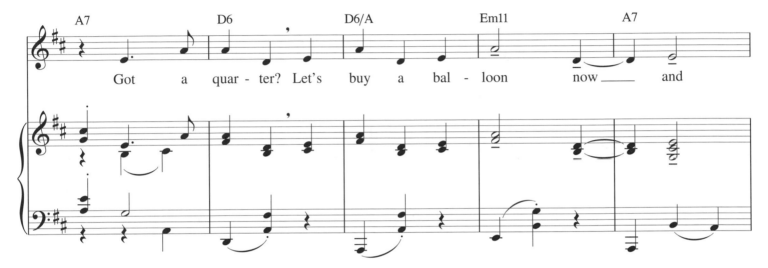

Got a quar - ter? Let's buy a bal - loon now ___ and

see it zoom ___ to the sky. Are you

hun - gry? We'll feast pret - ty soon now ___ on Cokes and

Low and Lazy

from the Musical Comedy Production *Sweet Bye and Bye*

Words by
OGDEN NASH

Music by
VERNON DUKE

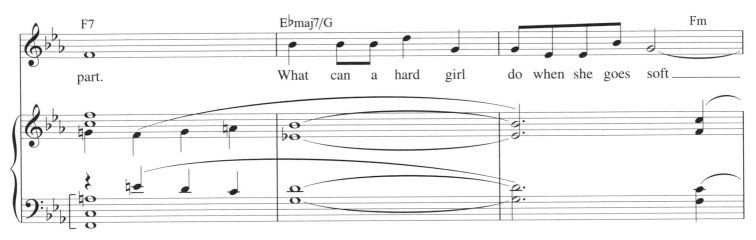

F7   E♭maj7/G   Fm

part. What can a hard girl do when she goes soft____

E♭   B♭m/G

____ but throw the rules a - way, What can she say, but

Refrain

B♭m6/G   C7♭9   Cm7/B♭ Fm7/A♭ E♭maj7/D Fm7/C Cm7/B♭ Fm7/A♭ Fdim/D Fm7/E♭

Low and la - zy, can this be me so low and la - zy,

mp – mf

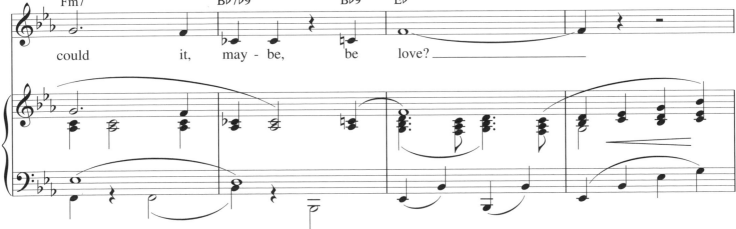

Fm7   B♭7♭9   B♭9   E♭

could it, may - be, be love?____

44

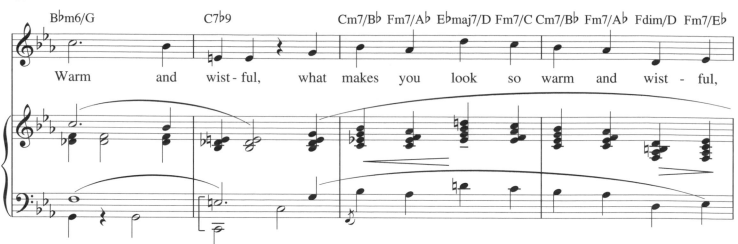

Warm and wist-ful, what makes you look so warm and wist-ful,

could it, may-be, be love?_____ There was

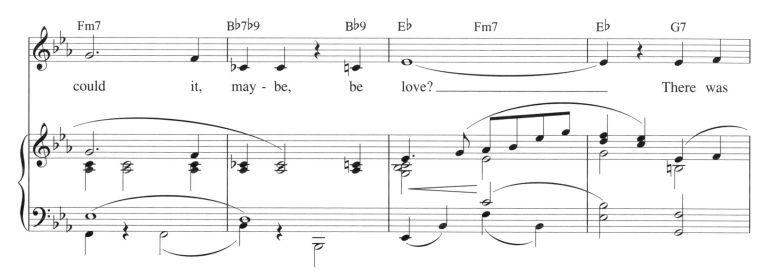

I who thought that hold-ing hands was sense - less, Now I'm de-

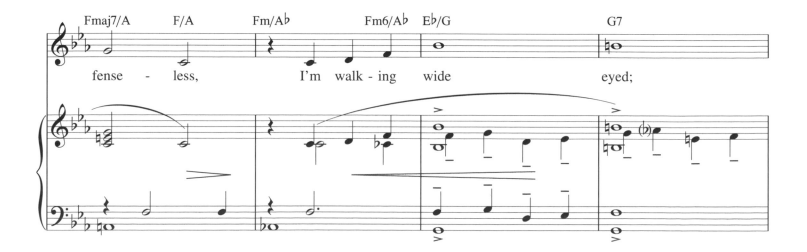

fense - less, I'm walk-ing wide eyed;

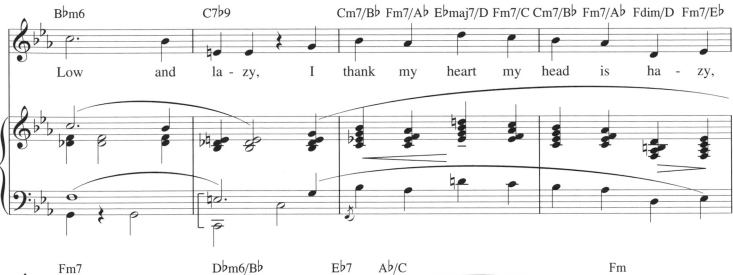

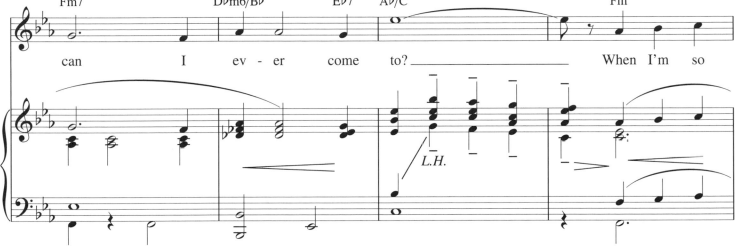

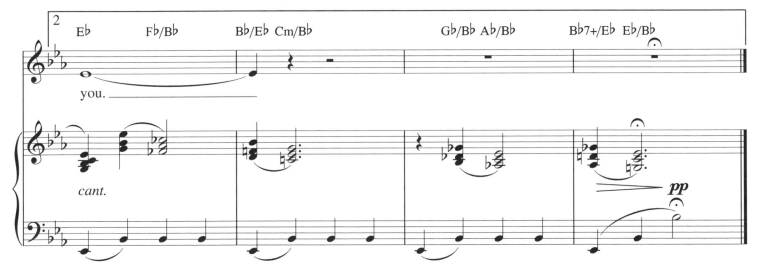

Madly in Love
from the Phoenix Theatre Musical *The Littlest Revue*

Words by
OGDEN NASH

Music by
VERNON DUKE

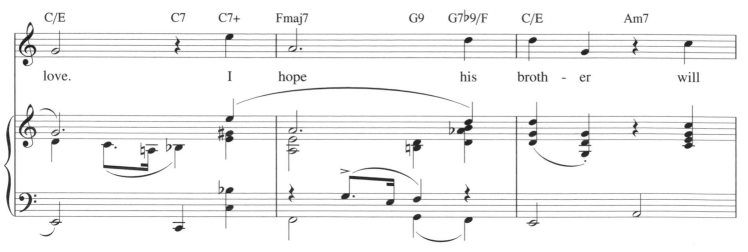

love.   I   hope   his   broth - er   will

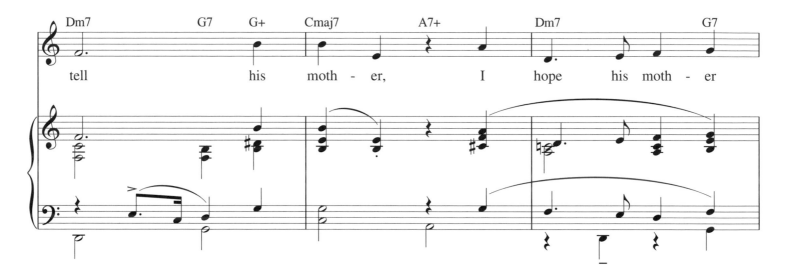

tell   his   moth - er,   I   hope   his   moth - er

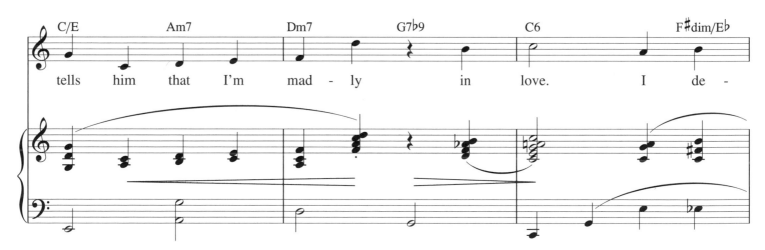

tells   him   that   I'm   mad - ly   in   love.   I   de -

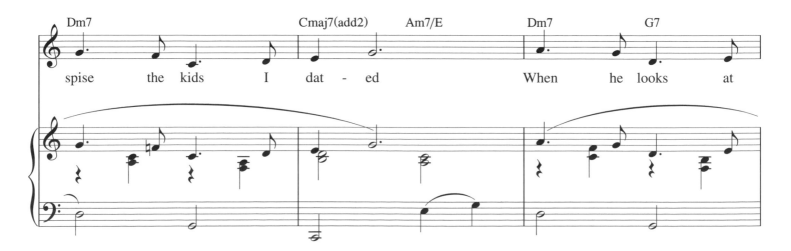

spise   the   kids   I   dat - ed   When   he   looks   at

Lyrics:

me, He's so - phis - ti - cat - ed, near - ly twen - ty - three. I think he knows me, Sup - pose he chose me, I'm old e - nough to kiss him and I'm mad - ly in love. His love.

rall.

p

Paris in New York
from *The Pink Jungle*

Words and Music by
VERNON DUKE

A Penny for Your Thoughts

from the Musical Revue *Walk a Little Faster*

Words by
E.Y. "YIP" HARBURG

Music by
VERNON DUKE

cal.   Just like that an - cient Bud - dha chink,

All you do is sit and think and think. A pen - ny for your

thoughts,   Al - though I know you may be wise. A pen - ny for your

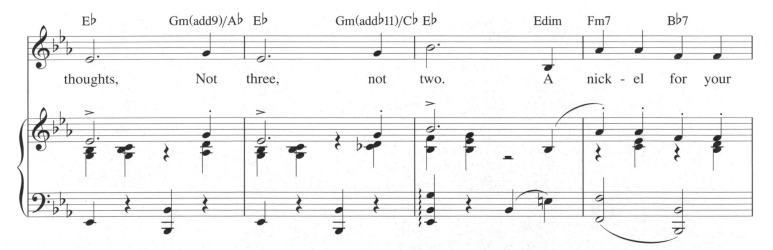

thoughts,   Not three,   not two.   A nick - el for your

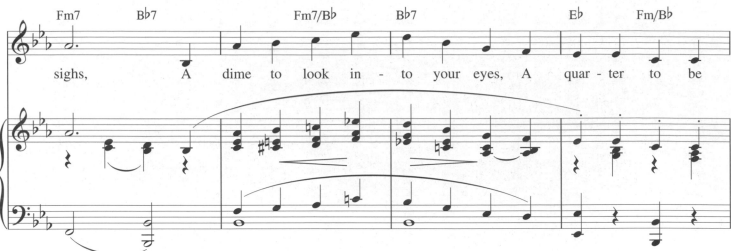

sighs, A dime to look in-to your eyes, A quar-ter to be

close to you. I'm the type who

goes for looks, And not for books, I'm prac-ti-cal that

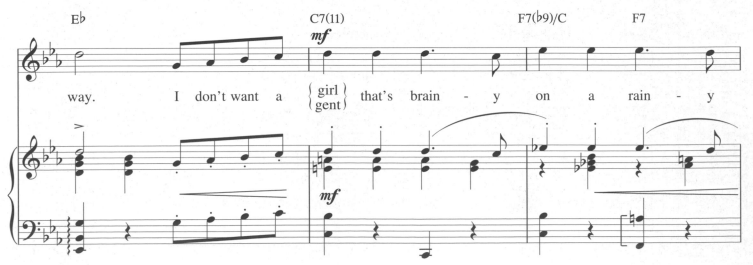

way. I don't want a {girl / gent} that's brain-y on a rain-y

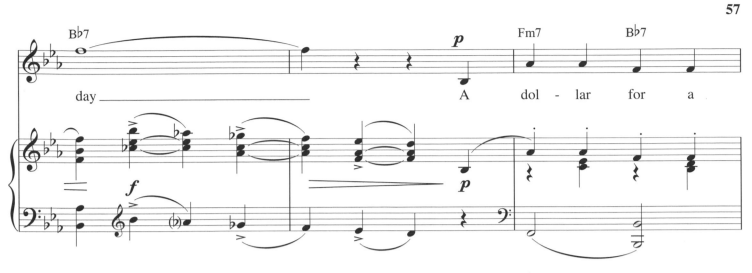

day _____ A dol - lar for a

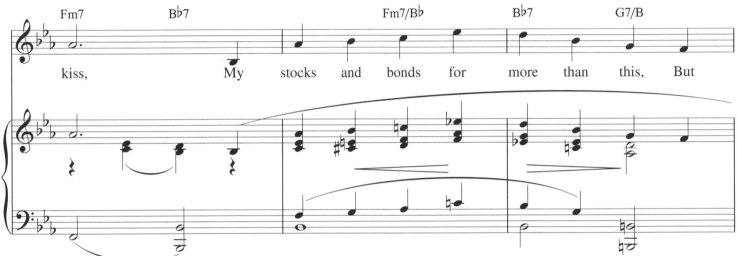

kiss, My stocks and bonds for more than this, But

just a pen - ny for your thoughts. _____

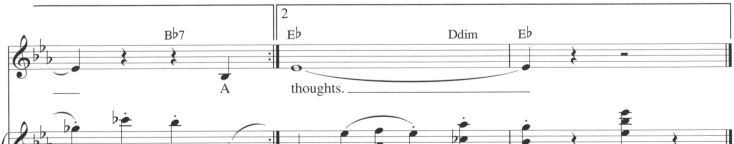

A thoughts. _____

This page left blank to facilitate page turns.

Round About

from the Musical Comedy Production *Sweet Bye and Bye*

Words by
OGDEN NASH

Music by
VERNON DUKE

Man is so lit - tle, and the world so vast;

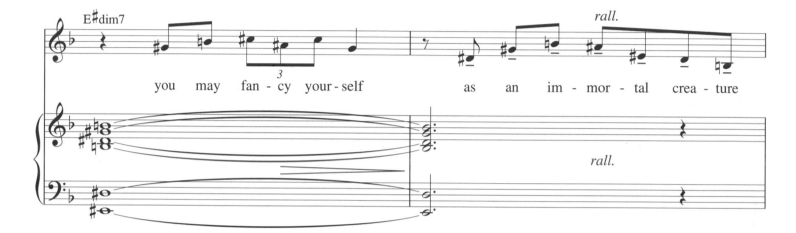

you may fan - cy your - self as an im - mor - tal crea - ture

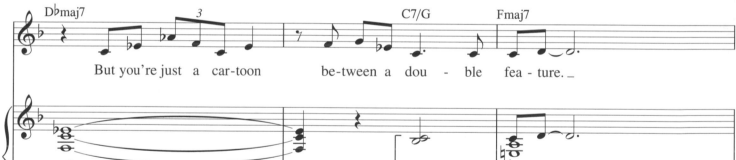

But you're just a car - toon be - tween a dou - ble fea - ture. _

Moderately

You go round a - bout and round a - bout and

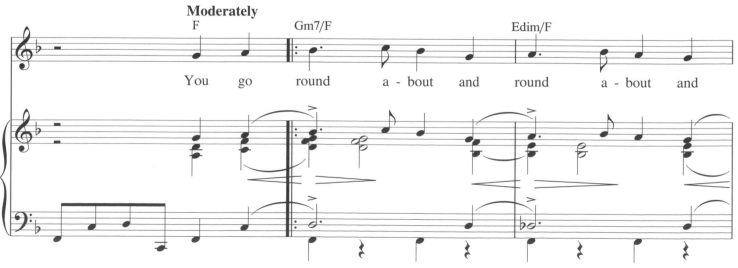

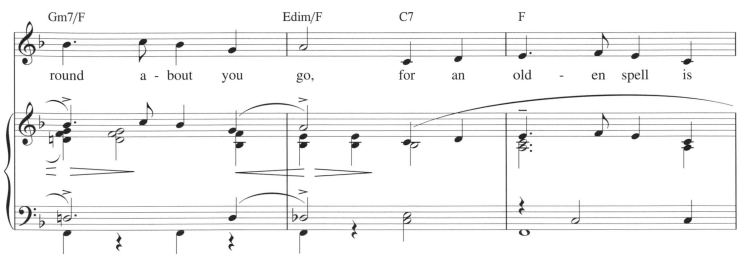

round a-bout you go, for an old-en spell is

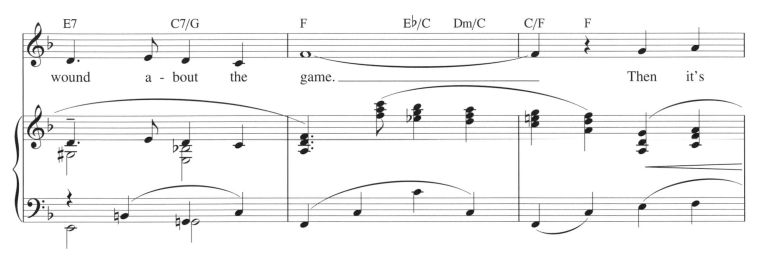

wound a-bout the game. Then it's

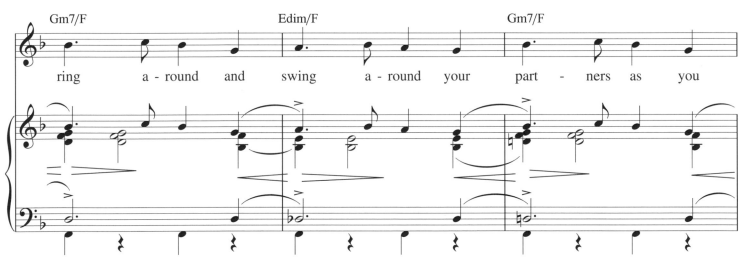

ring a-round and swing a-round your part-ners as you

go, but the more they change, the more they are the

63

Suddenly

from *Ziegfeld Follies of 1934*

Words by BILLY ROSE
and E.Y. "YIP" HARBURG

Music by
VERNON DUKE

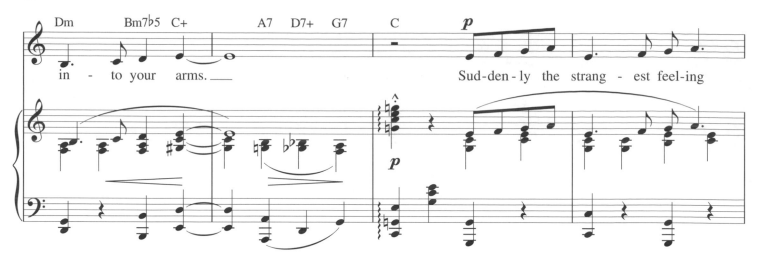

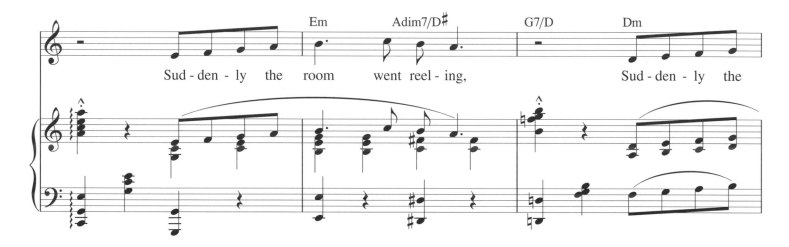

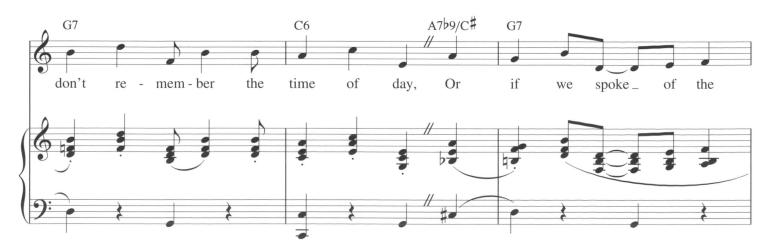

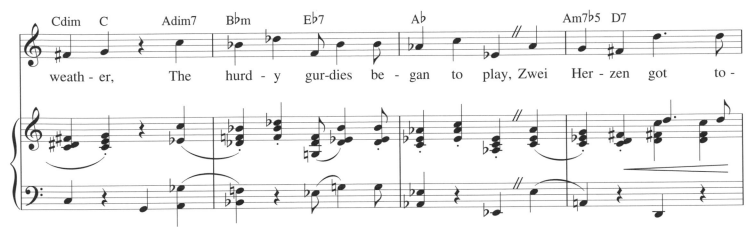

weath - er, The hurd - y gur-dies be - gan to play, Zwei Her - zen got to -

geth - er. Sud - den - ly with no pre - tend - ing,

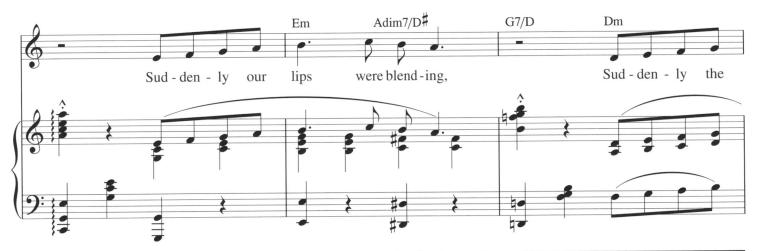

Sud - den - ly our lips were blend - ing, Sud - den - ly the

hap - py end-ing hap - pened to come true. true.

Sweet Bye and Bye

from the Musical Comedy Production *Sweet Bye and Bye*

Words by
OGDEN NASH

Music by
VERNON DUKE

What's the news? What's the word?

What's the time? Have-n't you heard? The fu-ture is just ter-

rif - fic and thanks to Gro - ver Wha - len ___ Man -

Clouds roll a - way, Let's grab the sil - ver lin - ing,

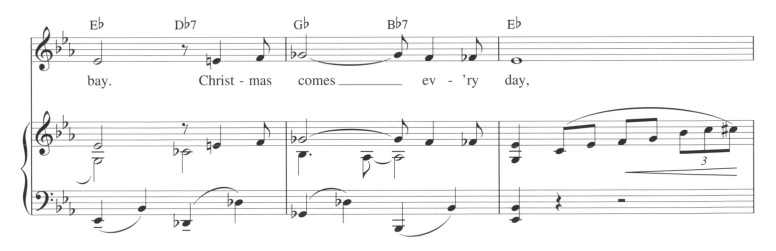

Here's your bou - quet, Our ship is sail - ing home up the

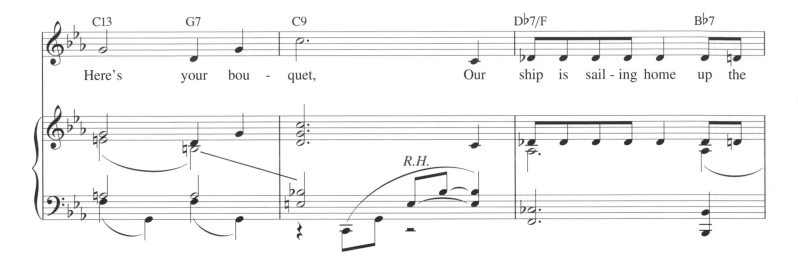

bay. Christ - mas comes ____ ev - 'ry day,

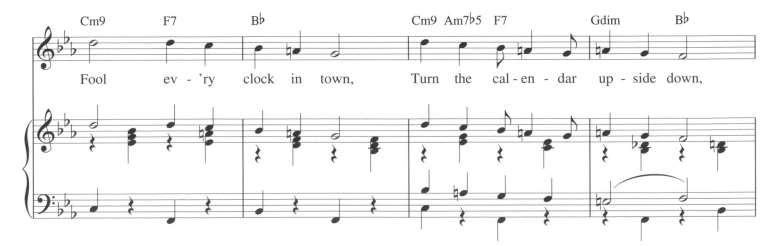

Fool ev - 'ry clock in town, Turn the cal - en - dar up - side down,

Eat our cake and have it too, Do it up brown.

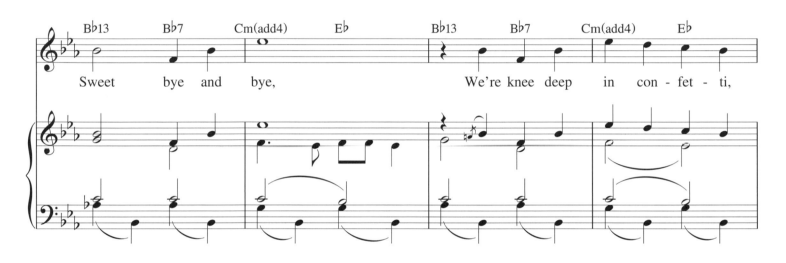

Sweet bye and bye, We're knee deep in con-fet-ti,

Rain turns to rye, There's cav-i-ar for all in the

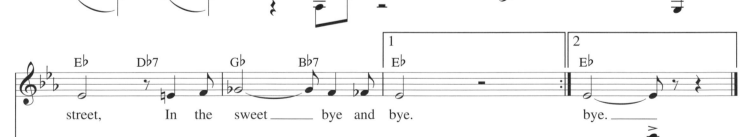

street, In the sweet ___ bye and bye. bye. ___

Published by Boosey & Hawkes, Inc.
229 West 28th Street, 11th floor
New York, NY 10001

www.boosey.com

AN IMAGEM COMPANY

ISMN 979-0-051-93424-9